Home and other Duty Stations

Home and other Duty Stations

Poems by

Emily Lake Hansen

© 2020 Emily Lake Hansen. All rights reserved.
This material may not be reproduced in any form, published,
reprinted, recorded, performed, broadcast,
rewritten or redistributed without
the explicit permission of Emily Lake Hansen.
All such actions are strictly prohibited by law.

Cover design by Shay Culligan

Cover Image/Illustration by Lacy M. Freeman

ISBN: 978-1-950462-83-4

Kelsay Books Inc.

kelsaybooks.com

502 S 1040 E, A119
American Fork, Utah 84003

For Lucia

Acknowledgments

I'm grateful to the following journals and anthologies in which versions of these poems were first published (sometimes under different titles):

8 Poems: "Brat in the Garden of Eden"
Anti-Heroin Chic: "Air Boss," "Blueprint," "Cycles," "Inheritance," and "Still Life"
Atticus Review: "Baptism," "Children's Pool," "Desert Vacation" "How to Feed a Sea Lion," "Postcards from Weeki Wachee I," "Postcards from Weeki Wachee II," "The Mermaid After Retirement," and "Why We Feed Him Tomatoes"
BARNHOUSE: "In the Rookery" and "Invasions"
The Camel Saloon: "Dismemberment"
Clementine Unbound: "Wild"
Dressing Room Poetry Journal: "The Shape of Our Bodies"
The Fertile Source: "Eggs"
Glass: A Journal of Poetry: "My male professor asks haven't women / been writing about this for decades already?"
Nightjar Review: "Apologies" and "BRAT"
Stirring: A Literary Collection: "The Escape Artist"
SWWIM Every Day: "Mirage"
Til' the Tide: An Anthology of Mermaid Poetry: "Before Weeki Wachee" and "The Sailor's Promises"

I'm especially grateful to *Nightjar Review* for nominating my poem "Apologies" for the 2018 Best of the Net awards and to *Atticus Review* and guest judge Paul Guest for selecting my poem "Desert Vacation" as the third place winner in their 2019 poetry contest.

I am in debt always to my teachers: Rachel Trousdale, who never gave up on a girl who turned in all her papers late, Alice Friman, who taught me to see, and the magnificently cool Laura Newbern, who might hate to be given credit, but who is the only reason I'm still writing today. Thanks too to Janet Dale who is the best champion and writer friend a girl could ask for and to Jude Marr whose work ethic and cheerleading consistently inspire me to keep at it.

Thanks also to my dad who framed and hung my first published poems as if they were photographs, to Austin for the void, to Bryan for the music, and to Betty who gave me back the desert.

My biggest thanks as always though go to Aaron and our boys—I'm so grateful to remake home with you every day.

Contents

BRAT   11

I

Mirage   15
Playing House   16
The Sailor Visits Weeki Wachee   18
Knife and Fork School   19
Children's Pool   20
The Sailor Returns from Deployment   21
Air Boss   22
In the Rookery   24
The Sailor's Promises   25
Our Father Who Art   26
Do Over   27

II

Postcards from Weeki Wachee I   31
Postcards from Weeki Wachee II   32
In the hospital you called a nuthouse   33
Blueprint   34
Before Weeki Wachee   35
Empathy   36
Wild   37
Dismemberment   38
Inheritance   39
The Mermaid after Retirement   40
How to Feed a Sea Lion   41
The Escape Artist   42

III

Birthplace	45
Superstitions about Moving	46
Steel	48
Why We Feed Him Tomatoes	50
The Shape of Our Bodies	51
Worry Stones	52
Apologies	53
Aubade	54
Eggs	55
Invasions	57

IV

Still Life	61
My male professor asks haven't women been writing about this for decades already?	62
The body is a house	64
Cycles	65
What is passed along	66
Geography	68
Baptism	70
Brat in the Garden of Eden	71
Desert Vacation	72
They say you can't go home again	74
Low Self Esteem in Your 30s	76

BRAT

I don't know what home is—a house
that doesn't spread between coasts,
a board game without missing pieces, a dog
that grows old in one place? I keep sifting
through the memories—the slog
of the pacific, the white sand
of the gulf—but what is home if you have
to remake it? At 40, my father pierced
his belly button in the kitchen. At 30,
my mother proclaimed she was a mermaid
stranded on land. I am waiting for my gills
to sprout, for this skin to slough off like a snake's,
but I once killed a cactus in its natural habitat—
I keep finding myself stuck in the desert
searching for sea.

I

Mirage

I learned to swim inland. Somewhere
in Maine my mother took me to a lake,
a round, sandy bottom thing shaded by trees.
We called it a beach as if we could make
it so by naming it. If we called it love,
then it was love. The first duty station
I remember wasn't even on a coast. There
it snowed in droves and we lived in a house
with green shutters. Or at least I think
they were green. My memory's broken
sometimes like a naval base without a sea.
My father told planes where to land,
my mother cried into her soup, I read
fairy tales in the closet and we called it
home. At the lake I swam out to a far
away dock. I cannonballed into schools
of minnows. I shivered in my pink suit,
the water cold like snow.

Playing House

1.

In the dream, it is white, two stories,
dark green shutters on each window, a half
memory of a house, the driveway littered
with snow, the inside empty, no blueprint
left for where the walls had gone or where
the snow would cake on the doorways.

2.

This house is skinny with a hill sloping
down to a small backyard. In it, a swing set
with one swing, silver pans for mining
mud piled high under the white cedars.
Inside, nuzzled beneath the staircase, a closet
with its very own door for opening and closing.

3.

Out back of this apartment, there are flowers—
sunflowers planted in lazy rows, purple plumbagos
with five separate leaves, native yarrow, wild roses.
Inside, a different type of flower: empty packages
of hair dye, empty boxes of microwavable fries.

4.

Here there are three full bedrooms, two baths,
the backyard a football field of pine needles.
The kitchen's full of needles too, spiny wooden legs
that separate eating from living, and above the sink,
a picture window lets in only the dying light
from the cal de sac.

5.

Inside this one, things are older: glass
doorknobs, locks that don't turn, windows
painted shut for safety. The glass is too thick
to break anyway, but the screened in porch
has tears in every corner. From behind,
fields swallow the house and leave
ancient, unmovable cannons.

The Sailor Visits Weeki Wachee

The sailor comes to this show every weekend;
he has his eye on the mermaid with the blue tail,
the one who seems the most like a real fish,
who smiles at the audience, but never poses,
never calls the tank a tank, it's always the ocean.
He met her once after a weekday show—
he was still wearing his dungarees and blue work shirt,
she was still pinned into her tail—
and he was sure that it was real lust. Back
at the barracks, he's making plans for her:
doodling little fish scales, holding
his breath in the shower, diving into the pool
without pinching his nose. Everything he owns
is beginning to smell like saltwater.

Knife and Fork School

To become an officer, they sent you first
to knife and fork school. I thought
they were teaching you how to cut
steak with a spork, how to eat cereal
with a plastic spoon or else how to drink tea
underwater like we tried to sometimes
at the hotel pool. The hardest part
was holding your breath. That summer,
having left one place already while we waited
for another, we moved to grandma's and ate cobbler
instead of dinner—unspooled tin biscuits
covered with syrupy peaches from a can.
For years, I thought it was something
no one could replace until one day
mom told me it was really nothing at all—
sometimes she'd add cinnamon, I guess.

When we visited you at school in Memphis,
we rode through downtown in a carriage
like they do in the movies: a speckled horse
attached to us by spindles and reins, the night air
sticky and lucid. We had last lived up north
and remembered nothing of humidity, of the way
the air could leave you stupid and wet.
My memories of that night end with sitting in a bar—
you drank cocktails with funny names,
someone gave me a shirley temple with extra
cherries. It seemed one way, but was another,
home in no direction, arrows pointing every way
you looked. You didn't need a knife or even
a fork to eat grandma's cobbler, a spoon
would suffice to scoop up the mush
of peaches and biscuits from the dish.

Children's Pool

We came expecting to see little children,
kids in sunhats, scooping wet sand into buckets,
burying their bodies underneath the sea earth.
Instead, we found fat seals, whole families
of the round, white creatures laying there
on the beach as if it were theirs.
A crowd had gathered around us to watch them:
the moms and dads and pups, all spotty and slick,
not dead, but still. From above the beach, they looked
like gray rocks with whispery white hairs.
I stood with my yellow bucket in my right hand,
pink ruffles on my suit. I watched my mom
watch them, the thirty or so seals she wasn't
expecting. I'd like to come back as one of those—
as the little pup at the center, sand stuck to his wet belly—
as something capable of catching her, of stilling
her for a moment, freezing her body in the hot breeze.

The Sailor Returns from Deployment

In my favorite photograph of us, you have
just returned from sea, still crisp in your
white uniform, a large hat balances
on your head. I am holding on
with every limb. While you were gone,
mom fed and clothed me, we had some fun
I can't remember, though it was mostly
turkey slices rolled into curlycues, microwavable
french fries served still in red cardboard boxes.
In the backyard of our base apartment, rows
and rows of flowers bloomed without our care:
purple plumbagos, red and pink geraniums
insisting on space we didn't have.
On the front porch, mom sat sometimes
in her bathrobe, the loose rope covering
the parts of her that had been taken.
She told the neighborhood kids she had once
been a mermaid and had left behind her tail for us.
What things did you leave behind that year?
Sometimes I slept in your t-shirts, my knees
glued up to my chest. You sent letters I still keep
hidden in a shoebox—evidence of love
I was waiting for to return.

Air Boss

Those weekends you wore a fancy suit,
your uniform traded for civilian clothes

I didn't recognize—though you woke early still
to polish your shoes as if on instinct.

I would get up with you those mornings
to sit in the garage as you ironed your jacket,

one hand smoothing out the creases,
the other smoking cigarette after cigarette

in the hazy morning air. Your job—they called
you Air Boss as if anyone could control air—

was to tell the show planes when and where
to land, to communicate through headsets

and hand gestures with the pilots up in the air.
I thought you were a magician then, orchestrating

tricks between layers of atmosphere. But
I skipped the last show you directed—

by then you'd showed me the den of screens
where you watched the blinking curlicues

of the planes. I knew then there was no
magic to you. The trick was hollow

like a log. The weekend of your last show
I stayed home alone instead, pacing

the empty halls like a bird above its prey,
like a rescue plane circling tragedy.

In the Rookery

We came to see alligators, to watch
their large bodies slunk in and out
of the water, to wait on tiptoes for one
to open its mouth, expose the rows of teeth
we're raised to be scared of. Instead
we found nests and nests of baby birds,
a village of egrets and spoonbills feeding
their young, resting on eggs, flying
above us without fear. You had tears
in your eyes as you watched them,
the pink feathered little ones fluttering
between swamp trees. I waited still
and earnestly for you to remember
the alligators beneath us, their thick tails
thumping against the dock, their mouths
agape in anticipation of the fall.

The Sailor's Promises

The sailor promised her things: gems
she couldn't get from the ocean, a chance
to travel the land, a clawfoot bathtub
where she could still, from time to time,
put on her tail. If she agreed, he told her,
his small blue eyes wrinkling, life would change
forever, for better, right away. His teeth,
she observed as he talked, were straight,
but soft at the edges, the bottoms almost round.
The front two bound together, it seemed,
by something foreign, a strip of resin, or maybe
plastic? It's wood, he tells her, tapping
the little space with his knuckle. Now
that he's said it, she can't stop staring,
fixed on the tiny part of him that's not real.

Our Father Who Art

As a child, I repeated the Lord's prayer
in my head so many times each night
that its words became nonsense
the way anything does if you repeat it,
the way in the storybook they stopped
believing Peter about the wolf—or was
it the wolf, not the boy, who was named
Peter? I read it too many times to remember.
It was you who taught me the prayer,
who sang it to me each night
like an incantation. Mom had sworn
off god back when the nuns slapped
her wrists with rulers, but you were a good
boy untouched by things like anger: your parents
stayed married, your town had one church.
No one taught me about religion, but I thought
your prayer would keep me safe like you did
sometimes when the winds changed,
when mom picked at my blackheads
in the fourth grade. But the prayer couldn't
stop you from leaving, couldn't fix my brain
to the right tethered pole. So I counted
bites instead, flicked on light switches—
if god wouldn't work, what would? Now
in your house when I need it, I'm a visitor
without prayer, no holy book hidden
in my suitcase. When you die, will I talk
to the ceiling again like it can hear me?
In the hospital waiting room, a monk
passes by me and I wonder if I'm dreaming—
who will believe me? would you believe me?—
when I tell them about his long brown robe
tied together with straw, his shaved head
round and speckled with age?

Do Over

If it's possible to return, you'll need to.
Get in your car. Head infinitely west.
Arrive in the evening, when day is petering
out with the theatrics of quotidian life—
that word I learned in French class,
but failed to use correctly. Don't stop
for pancakes or turquoise jewelry
in New Mexico. Drive past the flowering
saguaros in Arizona—I almost drown there,
remember? Yes, it's possible, you told me
when I had children, to drown in an inch
of water. You are looking for the coast.
Now head south, but stop before you cross
the border. Drive the winding streets,
slowly park the car on an incline—imagine
it's still the gray station wagon where I sat
in the back and doodled spirals on the blank
pages of your guidebooks. Don't forget the brake.
Can you see it now? Past the throng of tourists,
past the restaurants and that tiny art gallery
where you bought a portrait of a cardinal,
out in the grand distance: a moor of seals,
whole families beached together on the sand.

There I am: ten, in a red sweatshirt, sitting
on a wooden bench high above the beach.
My hair is too short—you liked it that way—
a thick headband holding back my bangs.
I am smiling, though without my teeth, and
I am scared: of the larger seals who slide
forcefully on their bellies, of the feeling of wet

sand, of the roar of the Pacific, that particular
sound of sea hitting rock, of the possibility
of getting wet, of what you might say if I did.
Now see me again. Watch me closer.
I am standing in the splash zone. I've walked
out along the narrow rock path to the sea.
I wait for a wave to knock me over. My shoes
fill with water and rest heavy on my feet.

II

Postcards from Weeki Wachee I

When the lights dim and the show starts,
there are three of them in the water, these
half women/half acrobats swimming
in a tank like sea otters at the zoo. The one
at the center has a coral bikini top that's supposed
to look like little sea shells, and her tail, pinned
together with tiny hooks at the back, is deep blue,
like the color of an actual ocean. She swims
in circles around the other two ladies, fast
as she can with her legs pinned together. The top
half of her body twisting and twirling, the bottom
half doing half butterfly kicks. The other two
tread water and communicate in hand signals,
gesturing along with the recorded story
that screeches on the speakers. They stop
frequently to huff in breaths from the machine.
But the twirling girl never seems to stop and grab
at the dangling oxygen mask, or if she does, she hides herself
behind the plastic sea rock. She must believe in the magic—
that while in the tank, her tail, fraying at the seams,
is a real part of her body, her waterproof blue eyeshadow
a real part of her face. It is only after she gets out
and the recording stops and the stage hand unfastens
the tail from her legs, that she breathes again,
believes she's human, sees the tank from above.

Postcards from Weeki Wachee II

One morning, my mother says she is mermaid, too,
and goes for a swim in our bathtub.

Each July, she drove us to Weeki Wachee
to watch the mermaids flip and twirl
and twist their bodies into pretzels and zig zags.
We counted the colors of their tails as they swam:
pink, purple, magenta, teal, and rose.
We imagined their stories, invented their princes,
talked forever about the shades of their hair,
how the brunettes seemed to sink
into the dark water, disappearing like a magic act.

In the hospital you called a nuthouse

you made trinkets: decoupaged scraps
of tissue onto little paper boxes, glued
together 100-piece puzzles, constructed
tiny birdhouses from prefab slats of wood.
You painted them when you were finished
with children's watercolors, dipping
brushes into water and then swirling
them across dots of cake paint.
Sometimes you made bracelets instead,
strung plastic beads onto rubber bands:
dark brown, light brown, black, circle,
circle, heart, circle, circle, square.

I wore it until it broke: the rubber band
bracelet you gave me as apology. One day
the band just snapped, the rubber so worn
down that it had become like flesh.

Blueprint

In my spare time, I make a house
of horrors, charge admission, spruce
it up with cobwebs, replicate the spider
that once bit me on the torso while I used
the spare bathroom in the hall. Red lines
spread out from the center, symmetrical
inversions like a child's painting of a flower.
In the bedrooms, I put in torture chambers,
BDSM whips and chains holding missing limbs
and fingers. Loudspeakers play the blues,
a hall of mirrors nearby to reflect the sadness—
circus ones where you always look fat.
In the main bath, a mermaid swims in a tank
of blood water. In the dining room, there's nothing
but onions and sludge. The coffeemaker
in the kitchen is broken—though the red light
still turns on to confuse you. Outside, you find
yourself naked in front of all your friends.
Someone videos you with your tits out
and whispers they're no good anyway.
If you try hard enough, it could just be a dream—
dead soldiers floating behind the house
on hologram horses. There's a pill you could
take to make yourself smaller. The exit
is in the corner. On the blueprint,
I highlight it in yellow, a point of egress
for those who still believe in escape.

Before Weeki Wachee

Before her life as a mermaid, she had other
lives, other jobs. Once, she managed a pizza shop,
wore a red checkered apron and learned
to toss dough in the air lightly like a beach ball.
Before that, she clerked at a motel, worked
the check out desk, had to wear black pumps
everyday. For a brief period—her favorite—
she was the Sunkist girl, walking along the beach
barefoot, samples of the orange soda balanced
on her right hand. The uniform was different
than a mermaid's: a pair of denim cut-offs, painted
toenails, an orange tank top hugging her flesh. They hired
her for her breasts, round, big, and young, and for that other
thing about her—the shine they couldn't describe.
People loved her. At the beach, men and women
circled her like bugs around a light, waited
minutes before asking for their ration from her tray,
their tiny part of her.

Empathy

It's hard to believe that once upon a time
as you went about your life—dusting bookshelves,
standing behind the check in desk at the motel,
watching rerun after rerun of Wheel of Fortune—
that your body nourished mine without thinking.
Maybe you thought all of motherhood would be that—
instinct and togetherness. Maybe that's why
one day in the car you lifted up your shirt sleeve
to show me your arm, the places you had cut
with a razor. At 14, at 31 was I created
to bear witness to your suffering?
I don't remember exactly what you said
when you turned your body sideways
that day from the passenger's seat to see me.
But I can imagine your face still, the yearning
in your eyes, for me to return inside
where I belonged, inseparable from your pain.

Wild

By the pool we drink from buckets.
You sneak in shots when I'm not looking.
Don't be a wet blanket, you say. But
there are rules I'm still uncomfortable
breaking. In the gulf later, you spot
a stingray and swim up closer. *Look!*
you point with glee at his clouded body.
I stay closer to shore, imagining
what one must look like in the wild,
if its fins seem like wings the way
they do on TV, if from your vantage,
you can spot the end of its barb,
if you can tell from closer whether
its mouth opens slowly or quickly
to catch the minnows beneath it—
does it even eat fish? Years back
at some sad sea park, I tried to get
closer. I wore a snorkel suctioned
to my face, green fins on my feet.
I took a step into the shallow tank.
All around me, rays swam about,
their fins overlapping into one gray
mass. The instructor said *go ahead.*
She pointed forward to the deeper
water, to the rays and sharks making
a home out of captivity. I watched
from the edge as if held there
by invisible strings—you planted them
long ago—unable to jump out, my legs
liquid and jelly. I mustered all
my strength to reach a finger out
and touch a spongy wing. It felt cool
and slimy, the residue like a word
on the tip of my tongue.

Dismemberment

After they took her tail, she had to learn
about feet: how to wriggle
the leftover thread out of her toes,
how to scrub off the dead skin
with a file, how to balance her weight
between the two of them—there were two,
that had surprised her. She became
meticulous, waxing away the blonde hairs,
fine and invisible, painting her toenails
red—a color the bottle called Red at the Beach.
Later, she learned to dunk them into water,
to tie them back together with butterfly kicks,
to move her toes so that each one
felt the ocean. At the beach now,
she sits at the edge of the shore,
legs spread apart, bottom buried in sand,
and tries to remember if she had been happier
back when she was whole and light
underwater or if she prefers this new work
of walking, heavy, through the waves.

Inheritance

In the new country, my grandmother
and her sisters carried their heads
like anchors, woven canisters meant
for immeasurable grain. One married
a different man for every decade of her life.
One's brain got erased by waves. One
wore a doll strapped to her chest for years
and years like a baby. My grandmother
planted flowers instead: zinnias and azaleas,
white magnolias snipped from trees.
She called them out by color, standing
in her nightgown in the daylight, her hands
perched like birds on her round hips.
She was sturdy in those moments,
a fat statue on her Florida porch.
But she was no different than the rest
of them: crazy women raising crazier
daughters, their Ukrainian names dropped
at the border. In college, I visited an exhibit
on genocide and cried like a baby. Where
does crazy come from? For years,
my grandmother's parents grew food
they couldn't eat. Rationing, they called it.
Punishment. My mother's sister beat her
when she went crazy. My mother swallowed
too many pills when she decided she didn't
want to live. I take Zoloft in the morning.
I drink too much beer. At the exhibit
there were pictures: bodies and bodies
and bodies that couldn't escape.

The Mermaid after Retirement

I really was, she tells them, *I had a tail right here
for legs.* The woman sits on her front porch in a bathrobe.
She crosses her legs at the knees, shakes pink slippers
off her feet, revealing toe rings and hairy ankles,
drops of sweat everywhere. But neighborhood children
gather around her like bees hovering around a flower;
she has stories to tell. She says to them, combing her hands
through invisible hair, that she used to be a mermaid,
that once she lived in the ocean with the fish
and made hair ties out of seaweed and tea cups
out of little round shells. The children sigh
and circle her like birds around a carcass.

How to Feed a Sea Lion

The sea lion, gray, skin like rubber rain boots,
works blind now. The trainer, who wears her hair
in a braid like a horse's and swallows her g's,
says he went blind years ago and had to stop performing.
Now, instead of jumping and splashing for an audience,
he swims with tourists, glides beneath their hands, twirls
and spins at the trainer's click, clap, click, snap.
He is older and slower, but still moves like a lion:
nose down, tail up, divine, diving and dipping
in the pool meant to feel, to him, like the ocean.
The ocean, he knows, feels in his whiskers—white
and pokey like an old man's, like a porcupine's needles—
is not here. I stand in the pool, my fingers gripping
the tail of a dead fish, and wait: for the moment
when his head will pop up from the water and his neck
will bend back and his head will curve straight up,
for the yelp he will sound, the bark from deep down
in his belly, before the click, clap tells him to grab
the fish between his teeth and swallow it whole.

The Escape Artist

On TV last night, after our son went to bed—his hair wet
still from a late bath—we watched a woman handcuff
and enchain herself and then jump into a pool as a stunt.
A clock counted the seconds as an audience looked on,
waiting for her return to the surface. I sat suspended
on the couch, wondering not if she would survive
or why she had done it, but how it must feel
to escape. You sat on the other side of the couch
fidgety, uncomfortable with her choice to purposefully
defy ease, to risk life even in the littlest way.
You like earth, not water—each day your hands trace
bits of matter under microscopes, each foot planted
solidly on the ground as you mow the grass,
pluck weeds from the garden bed, your biggest goals
in life to have another kid, build a shed. I'm the one
who takes our son swimming, who tries to teach him,
now that he's three, how to propel his body through the water,
how to paddle his arms, how to dunk his head under
and then stand back up in the shallow end.
I want him to know that water will bend
for his body, that he is capable of holding his breath,
of twirling weightlessly for whole minutes if he wants to.
It's you, though, who has the reoccurring dream:
drowning, your thick, long limbs reach outward
and then, like magic, you swallow the water
and find you can breathe it, can walk for hours
at the bottom of the sea. My dreams are unable
to conjure such escapes—often I am walking a path
I already know.

III

Birthplace

When I'm asked for my birthplace, I sometimes
forget and give it an easier name, assign
my arrival to a place I inhabit in memory.
I know I came late. I know the hospital
was ancient and dirty. I know my mother lived
alone afterwards for months while my father
sailed on a ship in the Medditearrean sea. What
was he doing there in the mid 80s no war afoot
I don't know except that he slept huddled
in a bunk the size of a coffin while I slept
at my mother's bedside, fused so closely
with her she got confused and thought
us still one. Did I miss him then?
When my grandmother arrived at the hospital
for my birth, she whispered under
her breath as if sharing a secret
with me before I was born *my dear,*
should we go someplace else instead?

Superstitions about Moving

The first time we stopped at Apache Junction,
the passageway at the start of the Superstitions,
we were just visitors, our jaws agasp
like everyone else's. We'd never seen mountains.
In the photo you took—me, wild-haired,
hands on either side of my face—
I am fat with euphoria, braced in the wind,
and ready. Behind my head, the mountain's
yellow peak—it was April, the cacti were blooming—
meets a serpent blue sky.

The mountains became the place to take
our visitors—your aunt, my mom, our friends
from college—all equally amazed at how
the Superstitions just popped up from the flat
desert floor, reminding them suddenly
of the existence of sky, the possibility of rain.

At the start of the trail of mountains,
across from Superstition's biggest peak,
a little gold rush buzzed, a tourist trap with gun shows
and ice cream. The last time we were there,
we paid a man ten dollars to see the desert's
most dangerous creatures: a scorpion
the size of a sand dollar, snakes with yellow
rings, a gila monster hidden beneath
a miniature mountain. From behind the glass,
they looked innocent, little artifacts
of desert life, just things—
they could never sting you.

We found them on accident: those superstitious
creatures and their mountains, red rock hills
interrupted by a crooked two-lane road that circled
the mountains like rope around a pole.
Signs flanked the roadway indicating
water: ahead Canyon Lake, Lake Roosevelt,
Lake Saguaro, blue bodies surrounded
by the brown and yellow desert.

For months, I thought they were just
mirages, things I'd only imagined possible,
until one day, we kept driving past the gold rush
and saw one: real water, blue, see through,
majestic, capable of being entered,
of entering us.

I had been ready to enter the desert,
to dig through sand with my bare hands,
to be an adult. Instead, I learned that cacti
only grow wild across the Superstitions
because they lie dormant in waiting—it seems
like they are always waiting—for the desert's
singular month of rain.

Steel

On the unfinished wall of our cold room
a family of spiders has taken up residence.

I flinch each time I open the door,
forgetting the persistent powdery web

stationed in the corner. The spiders scurry
from sunlight—fear goes two ways—

their bulbous bodies running for darkness.
I worry they're black widows, squint

to spot the red lines that might appear
on their backs, the ones you say distinguish

malice from innocence. And I should
trust you—once you silked widows

in a desert lab, your job to decipher
and replicate the elasticity of their webs.

There you saw the fangs up close,
learned that males don't produce venom,

began to trust that even the females
are docile without provocation.

I leave them be at your insistence—
though that doesn't mean I'm not scared

I'm scared of everything. You say
the silk of widows is as strong as steel.

Some nights I dare myself to run a finger
along the soft center of the web.

Why We Feed Him Tomatoes

At the new house, tomatoes grow in the side yard
in between weeds. We pluck them off lopsided vines
when they're still orange, the lush red tint
only beginning to fill in at the top. If you leave
them outside too long, the ants get them: hundreds
of sets of miniature legs crawl inside the fruit's skin,
microscopic mouths suck out the juice. Instead,
we line them on the windowsill in the kitchen
where they eat up chunks of afternoon sunlight and grow red.
We shovel them in plastic bags for visitors, a parting
gift from our home, and each night at dinner, we slice
a single one into tiny squares and trapezoids
and serve the pieces to our son. We say *Eat them. Remember?
You helped pick them* and watch as he chews
the spongy skin and tiny seeds between his baby teeth.
We wait for him to swallow. If he eats enough,
maybe, the dirt from this new place will sink
into his blood and erase the particles from other places.
This earth might eat up the other homes, the other earths,
the other planets that created him, strip his veins,
erase the biological matter and spare molecules
we can't touch from the outside.

The Shape of Our Bodies

My body is and isn't shaped like my mother's—
our breasts, yes, the same circles of fat unhinged
from the rest of the body, floating in a space
outside of us where we dare think *beautiful*.
Her mouth, I got too, the upper lip that curls inward,
the shadow space we paid to close between our front teeth.
But my body is and isn't shaped like my mother's—
her nose, a button, mine, a triangle, pointed
like a witch's, reaching out for air, for space
that hers—small, unattended—can't enter.

Worry Stones

I was once taken apart, my gallbladder
plucked from my body precisely with surgeon's
tweezers. It had filled with worry stones,
useless pebbles created with fat and lye.
On my belly, I bare inchworms as evidence,
wavy strips of skin recreated from the stitching.
They are fragile like all things I've recreated:
memory, broken bones, mix tapes of your favorite songs
I stirred with static. I once tried to remake home,
put the word back together with doll parts and string
and from each house create the definition.
But parts of me have been dismembered
and replaced with worry, dreads and rocks
that weight me to the bottom of a desert lake.
Moss grows where grass should be at our house now.
Green is green, we say. Tender and soft.

Apologies

If I were a man, I would have already
taken you. At the first sign of your kindness—
the first time you smiled at me on a lark—
I would have walked right up to you
because I wanted to and laid my hands bare
across your arms. But I was raised a lady,
told at eight about the blackheads on my nose,
at twelve about the particular wideness of my hips.
In elementary school, they weighed me in a line
and marked me red. I learned instead to swim,
to view water and the men who loved me
as exception. As an adult, I've tattooed
my skin as apology: here is art, it says,
I'm sorry you must look at my body.

Aubade

That night you stood balanced
on a precipice, my feet hung

in the dirt. For a moment,
I was overcome by the moon,

stopped you mid sentence to point
like a child at the orange sliver of light

in the dark summer sky. We stared
at it for whole minutes, the two

of us—married, adults—taken aback
by something old seen again new.

Is love enough once it can no longer
stop you like that in its tracks?

That night in a moment of elation,
you called me *a good girl,*

our bodies touching in the electricity
of daybreak. We watched the day

break, marveling and stuck together
by light. How do you turn away

from such a moment? I wanted to tell you
no, I'm bad, but found no words.

Eggs

I am learning to cook eggs: crack
them open against the pan, dispose
of the shells, wash my hands fast
under hot water, scramble together
the little round yolk and the clear junk
you say is called whites. For years,
I let you do the cooking, the messy
part, while I sat on the kitchen counter
silent, leafing through dusty cookbooks.

The first time I ate eggs, scrambled little
yellow things served with ketchup,
I broke out in hives, my whole body
suddenly covered in red, round welts.
My mother had to rush me to the hospital,
spent her first Mother's Day sitting in the ER,
running her fingers back and forth
across the new landscape of my legs.

For two years, I refused to serve our son eggs,
convinced that our casual weekend breakfast
would turn his body into a field of red hills.
When you finally fed him his first bite,
a fuzzy-edged square of your omelette,
I had to close my eyes. I watched
the welts pop up and grow, the red spreading
across his limbs, spearing his torso, crawling up
his neck like the ants that invade
his plastic picnic table every summer.

Three hours later, he is still fine, skin
white and smooth, milky as ever.
The welts just an invention, a connection
I've imagined and reimagined between us,
wanting to give him things I can't:
the lazy right eye I got from my father,
the lazy left ovary I got from my mother,
bodily things about us that can't belong to him,
bodily things about him that never belonged to us.

Invasions

Each summer sugar ants invade
the pantry—the half dug out room

where the drawers are lined in someone
else's parchment paper we haven't yet

replaced. The buggers persist
in the shallow seal of an oatmeal canister,

in the sugar I've tried putting in a ziplock,
in the red sauces we swear were unopened.

For years, wasps got in too through some
small hole above the window we tried to close

with masking tape. I would run out
of the room, my hands a flair at the sight

of one, its buzzing echoing into the hallway
like an oven timer or a nun. But over time,

I learned to cope. Some organic
cleaner in one hand, a blue glass jar

in the other, I entered the kitchen again
like a knight with a panic disorder.

Our son huddled in the hallway—*mom,
did you get it yet?* And even if I had

to lie—*nothing   will ever
        hurt you*—I always said *yes*.

IV

Still Life

Morning and the clocks have changed
and my sons talk apocalyptic—which way
would you pick to die? *The kitchen table
invaded by monsters.* Things are noisy
and it's still not dawn. Outside birds awake
too and I try to name them: wren and robin,
cardinal and finch, all early morning flit
and chatter. I grew up in quieter houses—
only the din of tv, the humming Santa Anna,
suppers with vegetables steamed of sound.
I crunched ice between my teeth instead
when I wanted something loud. What
I controlled then the same as what
I control now—nothing—
      and we're late for school
as always, my keys rattling in the lock.
In the car, there's an argument: *zombies
or daggers.* I pick falling houses, the wicked
witch crushed again under the foundation.

My male professor asks haven't women
been writing about this for decades already?

It's a crafted skill—I can undo myself
with a single   fleeting   thought.
I've got a potion good for rumination,
a shiny crystal in my pocket that pulls
compliments into secret   chambers.
No one likes an insecure woman.
And why should they? I pick flower petals
and they all say he loves me not. I pick
fruit and it's all rotten. I'm a spoil sport
when there's fun. I rain on parades
when I'm invited. But this is all
       whining
               who wants to listen to such
dribble? I come from a lineage
of women broken by potbellies
and oversharing. My mother asked me
at 8 if she looked fat in her dress.
My grandmother said the upside
of dying was that she finally got thin.
The first time a man really loved me,
I was shocked it wasn't a joke: *what do you call
a woman bound to failure by needlepoint
and crochet? A lady, of course.*
You sit her in the corner, you talk her
down to her friends, you position some
reflective surface perfectly so she can see
there's no escaping that *pinch of doubt*
planted as a chip in a computer, as a seed
inside dirt, as an egg burrowed in a uterine wall.

On my wildest days, I grow fibroids instead,
needy, incessant tumors that promise
they're not cancer. At night, they whisper
    this will only hurt a little—
        just stay still. I close my eyes
and imagine an ether without bodies,
a body without dimples, a dimple
unsevered by dog teeth. From his jeep,
a man jerks off to me when he thinks
I'm not looking. *But he didn't touch you,
right?*   No, he didn't touch me.

The body is a house

I could buy it neat checkered curtains.
I could learn to knit with steady hands.
My grandmother crocheted blankets
into her 80s, kept a sewing machine
on the kitchen table in place of fruit.
My mother can't sew a button—
and who am I kidding, neither can I.
But I could learn to make something.
I could fix things up with a little
elbow grease. I could wear clean
underwear every day. What a radical
idea—I could look in the mirror
and say nice things to myself.
Could I just call this body home?
Could I forgive it and live in it until
I bury it and could I love it even then
if no one else does?

Cycles

At the end of each summer the myrtles
in our yard shed their bark in rough curlicues
the way snakes lose their skin upon growing.
The ringlets get lost in the moss beneath them,
pools of useless tendrils. No one's ready yet
for raking—the leaves are green, the air
still incessant and wet—and so for months
they sit like lost things waiting for burial.
Is August the month for grief? It's too hot
to wear tights with this dress. At the funeral,
I cry for other people as if I haven't learned
how to be sad for myself. Our myrtles flower
only where sun has touched them directly,
the undersides baring no flowers and by
September one or two less layers of bark.
When I die, I want top shelf liquor. I want
French songs. I want someone to call me
crazy. When we return home, the shedding
is almost complete, the flowers all done
blooming, the bark disappeared into the ground
like wavy lines of yarn in carpet. I still know
nothing about plant life, am still confused
about things like the life cycles of frogs
or how bees take pollen and make honey.
When my children ask why the bark peels,
when they take the molting skin between
their fingers like batons, the only answers
I have are ones I make up on the spot.

What is passed along

Midway up, the panic starts
and our son—the younger one,
still little enough to be scooped up
with ease—is frozen, his fingers
gripped with superglue to the playground
ladder the way an infant gorilla
clings to its mother's chest instinctually.
Even his voice changes as he calls
for us, his miniature register—
his breath still smells like milk—shaking.

When we decided to have children,
I didn't think much about the things
we'd give them. When the younger one
was placed on my chest after birth,
his body still wet and bruised, I couldn't see
his eyes and so assumed they were already
brown, dark, earthly things just like yours.
I was shocked when you told me
they were blue. Now that he's older,
fiery golden circles surround his pupils.
In a zoomed in picture, I'm unsure
if you could even tell our eyes apart

though the circles come from
my mother. They don't belong to me—
what does? I watch him from a bench
and I wish I had better things to give him.
I want him to see that I'm not scared
as if my composure could unwind
our spiral of dna and bless him instead
with gifts of a god neither of us believes in.
There's more that I want for both of us—
my mother tells me during a fight

*all we can hope is to be better
than our parents and you're doing it.*

As a child, I watched from afar,
hidden behind some signpost
or bush, as my mother visited
the gorillas. A guide had once
told us that gorillas throw their dung
when they're scared and I was scared
all the time. Up close at the fence,
my mother whispered to herself *aren't they beautiful*
as the troop strolled about the hill.
What's nature and what's nurture?
I pull our son off the ladder
and hold him as tight as I can.

Geography

Each week at the bottom of the laundry bin,
I find lost things you've stolen as treasure:
bits of granite, beads meant for counting,
unlucky pennies you pilfered anyway
heads down. You see things I don't—
the white cat hiding in the neighbor's ivy.
Her eyes were blue, you tell me, *which
means she's deaf.* You memorize
these kinds of facts, want to know
for certain things I don't know at all.
After school, you tell me about the regions
of Georgia: Coastal Plains, Piedmont,
Appalachian Plateau. In the laundry room,
your stockpile grows, useless trinkets
laid out on a ratty metal shelf. I could
keep it there forever—we bought this house,
after all. You tell me it's in the Piedmont
region of Georgia. As a kid, I learned
about the Gold Rush instead, drank sarsaparilla
from paper cups on the playground,
dug for fool's gold in dirty sand. I took you
there once to show you the Pacific. You ran
into the waves with your new shoes still on,
returning soaked to your knees and smiling.
In California, we had to tell you, it's illegal
to pocket shell fragments or drift wood
from the beach and so for once you came home
empty handed. You didn't complain though—
you bought a pencil instead with your spare
change. Back in Georgia, I palmed

your leftover pennies while I waited
for the laundry. When it was done,
I brought the coins back to you and folded
your fingers around them as if they were
secret talismans, home a thing like dirt
you could hold in your hands.

Baptism

Where is the room where I can unpack
all my shit at once and be done? Where
can I lay out the geraniums and grief
and underwear on the floor and stomp
around power hungry like a watchdog
done with work? When I was born,
was I given a place of my own, and if so,
when did I lose it? I can't remember
the first town I lived in or the first room
I slept in or any singular moment
when I called for you out of love.
Did I ever? And if I didn't, why not?
A small child, in a garden of tall sunflowers
and weeds, was it then I realized nothing
grew if you didn't have a home? I routinely
kill the most durable plants now. I learned
nothing about botany or scripture. Once
though I got baptized in a hot tub, submerged
in tepid water in a crow's nest above
the church. You weren't there to watch me—
that year you lived in your bed—but I held
my breath underwater and saw your face:
paper teeth, button nose, a crown of hair
so jet black it looked fake. I was cold.
I wanted to go home. Later, I moved
to Arizona in search of warmth and found
scorpions instead.

Brat in the Garden of Eden

It got wild by accident—the clover
and crabgrass and dandelions growing
without permission. Our sons tiptoe
among them, maneuvering around
miniature strawberries we didn't plant.
Watch out for their red heads!
they scream in a cloud of laughter
and marvel. Each Sunday, we mean to chop
it down, to trudge the neighbor's borrowed
mower through our monster grass. We wanted
it to be clean and sparse—we like rules,
we drank at 21 in measured sips, you
a dark whiskey, me a red wine because
wasn't I a lady? But the clover is so tall
it's flowered now, fluffy white heads we pick
sometimes and place in slender vases
around the house. How do I explain
that the word home hurts when I read it
and that sometimes I imagine our yard
as Maleficent's magnificent fortress? Inside
we are safe enough to possess evil.

Desert Vacation

There it was suddenly—the javelina,
scurrying like a squirrel across the motel
parking lot. Its wooly body swerved left
and right around cars, darting towards
the conifers at the end of the row. You
gasped when you saw it—your face loud,
your mouth hung open in a squeal.
I thought something must be wrong,
the way you waved your hands about
at your sides, the way your legs froze
in the middle of walking, but it was just
joy, the desert pig digging up mirth
from your insides. I tried to chase after it
for a photo, speed walking with my hand
on the flash, but you stopped me, calling
out with caution as if I was the foolish one
and you were ever responsible. The picture
I managed turned out blurry and dark,
the javelina just a gray flash near the corner
of the frame. Who knew there was life
in the desert? I wanted to be able to prove it.
Long ago, I had lived nearby and slept
in a house where the oven was kept
in a breezeway outside. It was too hot
to cook then anyway and I burned everything
I touched. I came back with you looking
for home or for its opposite, for some sign
I had made the right choice. You took me
to a psychic. She laid out tarot cards
on the table, produced visage after visage
of sword and stone. *What's holding you back?*

she asked, pointing down to a knight
blocking the way. In the corner card,
a lady picked apple after apple from a ripe
green tree. I pictured the javelina, running
full speed on its tiny feet, its round belly
jiggling above the asphalt. *Nothing,*
I told her, my arms crossed against my chest.
Instead of a picture, I brought home a statue
as souvenir: an inch tall javelina, its body
recreated in slate and going nowhere.

They say you can't go home again

Off the interstate, I still knew
which way to turn: left and then left
again and finally right onto Davenport.
I was sure I would remember exactly
which house it was: a single story,
deep tan with dark shutters,
a seat in the kitchen with surround
sound windows. I wanted to show
my children that place, I wanted
to say here it is, I was once happy.
But as we made our way down
the street in the rental car, their feet
kicking up dirt on the seats, I couldn't
pinpoint the house: was it the first
or the second or the third one
on the street? There are places,
it turns out, you can't return to.
In Alameda, they closed the base entirely.
They sold the shipyard and the office buildings
and the apartment where we lived
to the city and now it rots—I imagine it
siphoned with cartoon cobwebs—lonely.
I tell my children instead

once upon a time,
I lived in a house with a sunken living room
and wide french doors that led to a patio.
I ran around a backyard with lizards
     and citrus trees   and real grass.
And beyond the wooden fence,
     there was valley

and sky,
hot air balloons dancing
every evening. Those red and orange ovals
lit up my view like planets
I thought I could reach.

Low Self Esteem in Your 30s

There's a point each January where I confuse
the camellias for dead. Their brown petals littering
the moss, I lament for a moment that they passed
that exact color red before I could write it down.
Not that I could have written it down—the red
somehow rose bright and not sentimental or ugly.
In February their color is always back and I am stunned
in a way that betrays me. In the mirror later, I stare
at my face, my eyes welled with tears, wrinkles
run across my eyelids, my chin droops downwards
as in winter. It is winter and I am stupid
for the longing. Did I miss it when I was rose red
and not sentimental or ugly? I want to travel
back and see, pick up all the bits of blemished skin,
nail clippings, rogue hairs, make of them something
reverse, whisper it promises *I will love you
this time around.* Plead with it *Let me do it again.*

About the Author

Emily Lake Hansen is the author of the chapbook *The Way the Body Had to Travel* (dancing girl press). Her poems have appeared in *Atticus Review, Glass: A Journal of Poetry, Stirring, Nightjar Review, Midway Journal, and Rust + Moth* among others. She received an MFA from Georgia College & State University and currently serves as the poetry editor for Minerva Rising Press. A 2018 Best of the Net Nominee, she is a PhD student at Georgia State University and spends most of her free time playing children's board games in Atlanta.

Made in the USA
Columbia, SC
24 April 2025